STAGE 3

DARE TO SUCCEED

BY STEVE COLE, ANDY BRIGGS AND JOANNA NADIN

ILLUSTRATED BY GIOVANNI POTA, JAMES GIFFORD, JASON PICKERSGILL, ANDREA ROSETTO AND ALEX PATERSON

OXFORD
UNIVERSITY PRESS

CONTENTS

VOYAGERS
TO THE
STARS!

BY STEVE COLE
ILLUSTRATED BY JASON PICKERSGILL

Setting the scene

A voyager used to be someone who went on long sea journeys and explored new places. But what about exploring in space? Who, or what, would go on a voyage of discovery to explore distant planets millions of kilometres away from Planet Earth? Find out by reading this text ...

VOYAGERS TO THE STARS!

What lies out there in space? The question has tantalized human brains for thousands of years. Yet it wasn't until the 20th Century that we could finally send explorers into space. Although humans have walked on the moon, our mechanical explorers have travelled much further than that.

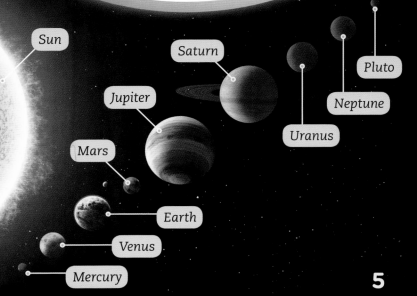

Sun

Saturn

Pluto

Jupiter

Neptune

Uranus

Mars

Earth

Venus

Mercury

5

Launching Voyager

In 1977, the space probes *Voyager 1* and *Voyager 2* were fired into space. They were designed to fly past Jupiter and Saturn, the biggest planets in our solar system, and send pictures and information back to Earth.

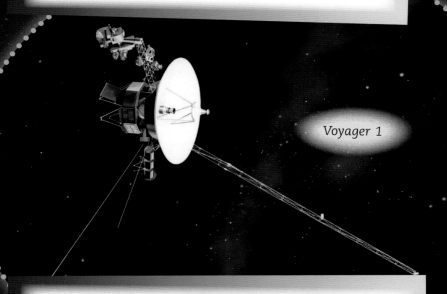

Voyager 1

Each Voyager was carefully launched on a different **trajectory**. *Voyager 1*'s path would take it to Jupiter, then out past Saturn's rings and its moon Titan, exploring them close-up. It would then travel outwards from the solar system to explore **interplanetary** space.

Voyager 2's path would take advantage of the planets of our solar system being 'lined up' in a row (this only happens once every 175 years). It would visit Jupiter and then use Saturn's gravity to speed it on its way to Uranus, and Uranus's gravity to speed it on to Neptune before leaving the solar system.

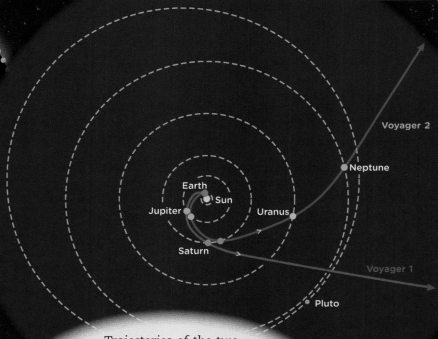

Trajectories of the two Voyager space probes. Some planets are shown twice, as their positions changed between the launch of the two voyagers.

Out into space

Jupiter

The Voyager probes discovered some astounding things about Jupiter. They found a set of faint rings around the massive planet, and volcanoes erupting on one of its moons – the first active volcanoes ever found on another world!

Voyager 1 image of the ring around Jupiter, marked with the white line. The ring is estimated to be about 30 km thick.

Saturn

After leaving Jupiter, *Voyager 1* reached Saturn in 1980, three years after its launch, while *Voyager 2* followed in 1981. The probes sent back thousands of photographs of the planet, its rings and its many moons – and discovered even more moons than had previously been known about.

Saturn with some of its moons, 4th August 1982

Uranus

Having explored Saturn, *Voyager 1* was thrown off on a new trajectory into outer space, while *Voyager 2* zoomed further out across the solar system at 64 000 km per hour. It reached Uranus in 1986, and discovered ten new moons, as well as **charting** the five already known to exist. The moon Miranda was found to have a patchwork of different surfaces, with **chasms** nearly 20 km deep.

Uranus's moon Miranda

Neptune

In 1989, *Voyager 2* reached Neptune, the outermost planet. Five new moons were discovered there, four rings were counted around the planet and a mass of information was gathered about this distant, freezing world. For instance, winds on Neptune are the strongest in the solar system, nine times stronger than the strongest winds on Earth.

Neptune's Great Dark Spot, a huge spinning storm with winds up to 2400 kph

Interstellar space

Illustration of *Voyager 2* leaving the solar system

After leaving Neptune, the Voyagers' planetary missions were over. However, their work still goes on. Both space probes are now far further from the Earth than Pluto is. *Voyager 1* has entered **interstellar** space, where the sun has no power, and no one and nothing from Earth has ever been. *Voyager 2* is set to follow it out of the solar system in a different direction.

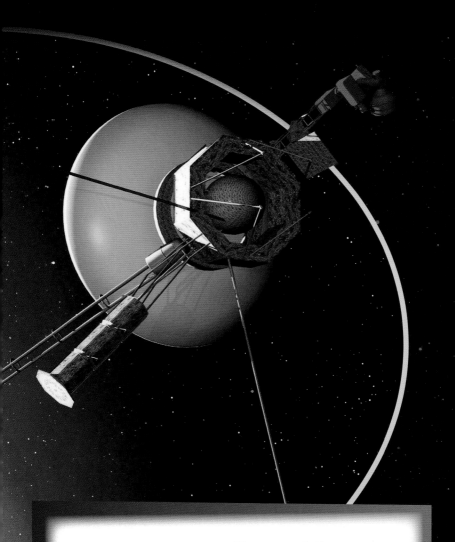

Both Voyagers are still transmitting scientific measurements of their surroundings back to Earth. However, by 2025, the Voyagers will be out of power and unable to operate ... truly lost in space!

Time capsule

The Voyagers each contain a time capsule – a golden disc of sounds and images from Earth.

Back in 1977, the president of the United States recorded a message to be carried by the Voyagers, in case aliens ever found them: "This is a present from a small, distant world, a token of our sounds, our science, our images, our music, our thoughts and our feelings. We are attempting to survive our time so we may live into yours."

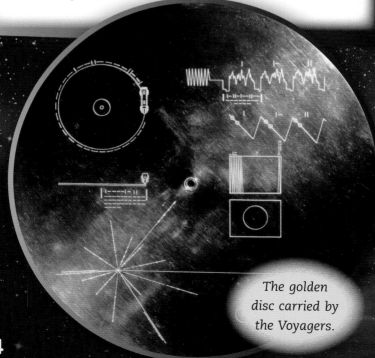

The golden disc carried by the Voyagers.

Remember, every star we see in the sky is a distant sun and may have planets of its own. Perhaps one day, an alien living on one of those planets will find *Voyager 1* or *Voyager 2*, look inside and learn all about us, so far away on a tiny little speck called Earth.

Then, maybe – just maybe – they'll come to visit …

Glossary

chart	to make a map of something
chasm	a deep crack in a rocky surface
interplanetary	between the planets
interstellar	between the stars
trajectory	a pathway

INVASION FROM SPACE

BY STEVE COLE
ILLUSTRATED BY GIOVANNI POTA

Setting the scene

Imagine that it is hundreds of years in the future and humans can live on planets and moons all over the solar system. Travelling is easy, thanks to the teleporter that can send you unimaginable distances in a matter of seconds. This is the world that Binka and Jello have grown up in.

Chapter 1

"Come on, Jello!" Binka yelled upstairs. "We'll be late for school."

"Don't think so, sis!" Jello came floating downstairs on his hover-boots. "We've still got one-and-a-half minutes until lessons start – and the telepod will zap us over to Pluto in thirty seconds." He whooshed past her. "Come on, then!"

Binka shook her head wearily and followed him to the telepod.

The majestic blue disc of Neptune shone in through the window. Binka barely noticed – she'd seen the same view every day of her life. For thirteen years she'd lived here on Triton, Neptune's largest moon – but these days, thanks to the telepod, it didn't matter where you lived. You could travel anywhere in the solar system in next to no time.

"Can you believe that people used to use space rockets?" Jello laughed as he programmed the telepod to take them to school. "It took years to get *anywhere*."

Things were very different here in the year 2300, thought Binka. The telepod might look like a shower cubicle with glowing lights, but it projected you safely across millions of kilometres. She and Jello had gone to nursery on Mercury, junior school on Mars and now attended secondary school on Pluto – along with 20 000 other kids!

"Right!" said Jello. "Travel starts in ten seconds."

Binka stood next to him and yawned. Travel by telepod was so boring. You just zapped from one place to another in a moment, with no sensation–

WHOOOOOOOOOSH!

"Whoa!" Binka shouted, as the telepod shook and blue sparks spat wildly all around. "What's happening?"

Warning letters filled the telepod's main screen: POWER SURGE!

"Ow!" Jello yelled, his hover-boots smoking. "My feet are on fire!"

Binka felt the world spin about her. Then the telepod's door swung open.

She gasped at what she saw.

It was not the travel room at home. It was not the landing bay at school.

It was a black metal room: cold, dark and empty.

"I'm sorry!" Jello groaned. "I forgot to turn off my hover-boots. They run on high-energy cells – I bet they caused the power surge!"

Binka scowled at him. "Something certainly scrambled the controls and made your hover-boots go up in smoke." She hit the recall button on the telepod's controls, but all the screen said was ERROR.

"Oh, well. This beats a normal day of star-school!" Jello grinned at his sister. "And don't worry about my hover-boots – they're self-repairing! They'll be fixed in no time."

"I only hope the telepod will fix itself as quickly," Binka frowned. "Meanwhile, let's see where we are."

A gloomily-lit corridor stretched out ahead of them. The walls were black and spongy, the floor and ceiling were crimson. The hum and pulse of hidden control systems throbbed about them and a foul, rotting stench filled the air.

"This place stinks like a monster's armpit," said Jello, holding his nose. "How far through space did that power surge throw us? We're lost! Lost in space ..."

"Maybe we can tell where we are by the stars," said Binka. "Look, here's a window."

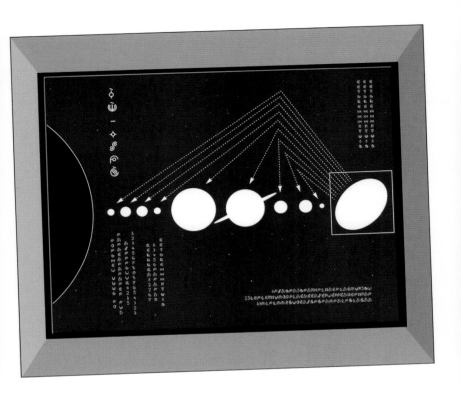

It wasn't a window, though. As they both took a closer look, they realized that it was a screen that showed a map. On the right of the screen was an object the shape of a rugby ball. To the left, were nine dots in a row next to a large yellow circle. Red arrows were flying from the rugby ball to all of the dots.

Jello frowned. There was something about the size and position of the dots that he recognized. "Does that look familiar to you?"

"It's ... it's the solar system!" Binka gasped. "That big circle is the sun. There's Neptune, and Pluto ..."

"Look – we must be stuck on the dwarf planet, Haumea." Jello pointed to the rugby ball. "We've jumped more than six million kilometres! But what do you think the red arrows are?"

He tapped the map and the red arrows began to move, like in a cartoon. They swooped and jabbed into the dots, which started to smoke and burn.

"This isn't just a map." Binka felt a prickle along her spine. "It's more like a *plan*. A plan of attack."

"Attacking the whole solar system!" Jello felt his knees turn to jelly. "But whose plan is it?"

As he spoke, a huge, lumbering, blue creature stomped into sight at the end of the corridor. It looked like a reptile, with long clawed arms and two tails. Its scaly face was dominated by one huge red eye – an eye that narrowed at the sight of the intruders.

"Er ... I'm guessing it's *that* thing's plan!" said Binka.

With a fearsome roar, the creature charged towards them.

INVASION FROM SPACE
Chapter 2

Chapter 2

Binka and Jello stared in horror as the blue creature pounded closer.

"SPIES!" It bellowed. "HERE IN WAR CENTRE ... JUST BEFORE WE LAUNCH INVASION!"

"Run!" Binka turned and pelted away along the corridor, dragging Jello after her. They ran for what felt like forever.

"I wish my hover-boots' automatic repair system worked faster," Jello panted. "I could whoosh along faster and give you a tow."

"I wish we could whoosh to Triton right now," Binka gasped. "Somehow, we have to warn everyone back home."

The reptilian creature was still lumbering after them, its long claws scraping the floor.

Binka skidded to a stop in front of a door. "Let's give it the slip." She slid the door open ... and froze. It led to a control room, full of weird, bulky machines, glowing with alien light – and six more of the big, blue aliens! Luckily, they did not turn round. Five were busy at their controls. The other alien stared out through a large window onto an icy plain.

"Quick," said Jello. "Let's hide!" Just in time, he and Binka ducked behind a bank of controls as the alien chasing them burst in.

"HUMAN SPIES IN HERE?" it snarled.

Jello and Binka held their breath.

"DO NOT INTERRUPT!" roared the alien at the window. "WE ARE ABOUT TO TELEPORT THE ARMIES."

"ALL SET FOR SENDING," one alien reported. "PLATOONS ONE TO FIVE WILL TELEPORT TO EARTH. PLATOONS SIX AND SEVEN TO MARS. PLATOONS EIGHT AND NINE TO TRITON ..."

The alien at the window laughed. "WE SHALL STOP HUMANS SPREADING THROUGH SPACE ... FOR GOOD!"

Jello peeked out to look through the window. His stomach turned like a tangle of comets. Outside were literally thousands of blue aliens in silver armour, standing in squads that stretched into the distance. In their many claws they carried tubular weapons and blood-red scimitars. It was a terrifying sight.

"Just look at them all," Binka whispered. "Alien soldiers ready to make surprise attacks all over the solar system."

"The aliens must have their own telepods," Jello hissed. "Instant invasion. Our people won't stand a chance!" Suddenly, his hover-boots made a loud chiming sound. "Hey!" he beamed. "They're fixed!"

At the sound, every creature in the room turned to stare at them. Seven big red eyes narrowed with malice.

The alien in the doorway pointed at Jello and Binka. "THERE!"

"SPIES!" hissed the alien at the window. "GET THEM!"

"Time to go!" cried Jello, hitting a switch on his hover-boots. He rose into the air and lifted Binka with him. They whizzed at top speed over the alien in the doorway, Binka clinging on to Jello with all her might.

A loud alarm boomed out in the corridor, and as Binka looked behind she gasped with horror. A whole horde of the creatures was after them!

"Where can we go?" she groaned.

"I'll tell you where," said Jello. "Straight back to that control room."

Turning sharply, he went zipping towards the onrushing aliens! They snatched at him and swiped at Binka but Jello pulled an Olympian array of dazzling mid-air stunts, and the hover-boots boosted both him and his sister past the lethal claws.

Back in the control room, a single massive alien now stood at the controls. "ALL SYSTEMS FULLY CHARGED," it announced. "BEGINNING TELEPORT SEQUENCE ..."

"No way!" Binka shouted. "Jello – put the boot in!"

"I'll put *both* in!" Jello cried. Then he landed heavily on the controls with his hover-boots, just as the alien pressed the ACTIVATE button. Blue sparks exploded from the console, dazzling the alien, as Jello and Binka backflipped away and whooshed out of the room.

"NOOOOOOO!" they heard the alien cry. "TELEPORT UNSTABLE ... DESTINATIONS SCRAMBLED ... PLATOONS SCATTERED THROUGH SPACE!"

"You and your boots have done it again!"
Binka cheered, as the hover-boots propelled
them along the corridor.

An even louder alarm started up, and a gruff
voice rang out: "ALERT! REMAINING CREW
TO SPACESHIPS AT ONCE! WE MUST
RESCUE OUR STRANDED SOLDIERS!"

"Sounds like these creatures will be busy for a while." Jello steered back inside the storeroom where the telepod had landed. "Let's hide out here. The moment the pod's auto-repair systems have finished their job, we can travel straight back home and warn everyone about these monsters."

"We have the co-ordinates for this base in the pod, so our star-troops can come here fast and stop them," Binka said, wiping her brow. "I just hope they tell our teachers we're heroes ... or else we'll probably get a detention for missing school."

"A detention – for saving the solar system!" Jello grinned. "Wouldn't that be just our luck?"

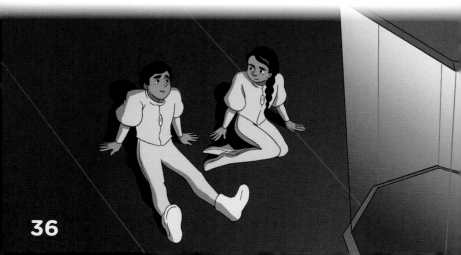

CRASH LANDING

BY ANDY BRIGGS
ILLUSTRATED BY JAMES GIFFORD

Setting the scene

Picture the scene: the wreckage of a space-craft is half buried in the desert and parts of it are still burning. Two children dressed in spacesuits are lying, unconscious, on the ground. What sort of story begins like this?

Chapter 1

Baxter was the first to wake up, and he regretted it instantly. His head felt as if somebody was using it to play the drums, but that wasn't as surprising as the burning wreckage of a spacecraft that surrounded him.

His sister lay beside him. They had both been flung clear of the crashed craft which lay three hundred metres away, thick plumes of black smoke pouring from it.

"Amber, are you OK?" Baxter shook his sister, fearing the worst. He was relieved when she coughed and slowly sat upright to take in their surroundings.

"Where are we?" Amber murmured.

Baxter shook his head. He couldn't remember anything about the impact. One moment they had been cruising through the solar system as usual; the next, waking in this alien land.

"This is the escape pod," Amber said, nodding towards the wreckage. "Does that mean the rest of the ship is still in orbit? Or ..." She dreaded finishing the sentence.

Neither of them could completely recall why they were travelling across the solar system. Were their parents with them? Or had the autopilot been guiding them onwards?

"This doesn't look like any planet I've seen before," Baxter said as he stood up. He wobbled slightly but was relieved that they both seemed unharmed.

The rugged landscape was barren, dotted with huge thorny bushes poking from the rocks. In one direction, dark, jagged mountains lined the horizon like bared teeth, twin orange suns poised in the sky. Behind them it looked as if the trees blossomed into a forest of red leaves. There was no hint of civilization in any direction.

Baxter nodded towards the trees. "I reckon we head in that direction and see what we can find."

A quick search of the wreckage revealed nothing of use. Baxter took a piece of metal from the wreckage, thinking it would help fend off any aggressive alien life. Amber found an old sweet wrapper and a blank blue circular token in her pocket.

They headed towards the distant treeline, walking in silence, neither of them daring to guess why they were marooned on an alien world.

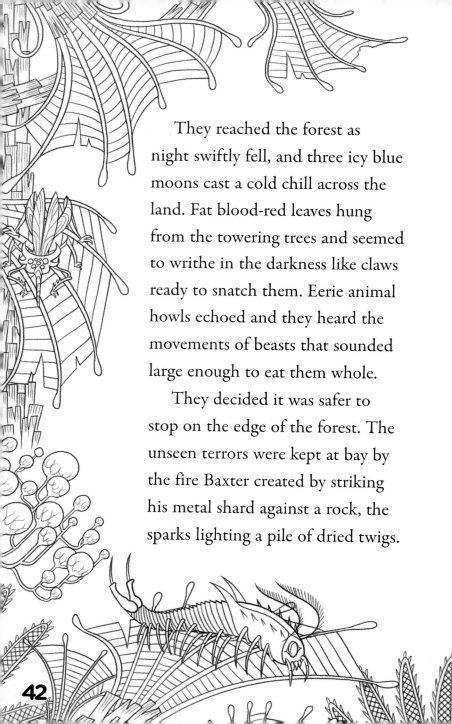

They reached the forest as night swiftly fell, and three icy blue moons cast a cold chill across the land. Fat blood-red leaves hung from the towering trees and seemed to writhe in the darkness like claws ready to snatch them. Eerie animal howls echoed and they heard the movements of beasts that sounded large enough to eat them whole.

They decided it was safer to stop on the edge of the forest. The unseen terrors were kept at bay by the fire Baxter created by striking his metal shard against a rock, the sparks lighting a pile of dried twigs.

They sat close to the fire for warmth, trying to ignore the chilling squeals the twigs made as they burned. As Amber stared into the flames, a memory popped into her mind. "Do you remember the story Mum used to tell us at bedtime?"

Baxter frowned. "The Fable of the Screaming Forest?"

Amber prodded the fire to keep the flames alive. "That's the one. It reminds me of this place."

They peered into the darkness and told each other the tale. It helped calm them and, despite their grumbling stomachs, tiredness overcame them and they both drifted to sleep.

With sleep, the vivid dreams came.

The harsh sound of a warning klaxon rang out as Baxter and Amber sprinted down a bright white corridor that shook around them. The ship's computer spoke in a calm voice. "Imminent asteroid impact!"

Baxter shoved his sister into the escape shuttle and looked around in panic.

"Mum! Dad!"

His parents appeared at the far end of the corridor, their faces masks of terror as the ship shuddered around them.

"Go!" his father yelled. "We'll use the second pod! Amber, use your token—"

A sudden explosion punched through the corridor between them as an asteroid struck. The impact hurled Baxter into the escape pod.

With a sudden jolt, Baxter awoke. He sat bolt upright, before realizing he wasn't in the escape craft but lying in the dirt at the edge of the forest. His heart hammered in his chest as his memories of flying into the asteroid belt returned. Their parents had been with them! Now the question was: had they managed to crash-land safely too?

Baxter reached over to wake Amber – but his hand froze in place. In the darkness beyond her, something moved. Something large and deadly. Its deep growl warned him that any movement would be their last …

Visit the GELOPOLIS SYSTEM

BY ANDY BRIGGS

ILLUSTRATED BY ANDREA ROSETTO

Setting the scene

What would it be like to be a tourist in space? This text is a tourist brochure all about a group of planets called the Gelopolis system. The aim of the brochure is to persuade people to have holidays there. The only problem is – each planet is extremely dangerous! Would *you* dare to visit?

Visit the
GELOPOLIS SYSTEM

Have you ever wondered what marvels await you in the amazing twin-sun GELOPOLIS SYSTEM? Well, wonder no more – start exploring today!

This newly-opened region on the edge of the galaxy has it all, making for an out-of-this-world adventure holiday destination!

In the past, these planets were off-limits due to the extreme dangers found there. But now you can travel with the peace of mind that almost nothing is likely to happen to you*. And if it does – it's all part of the adventure! Talk to your interstellar travel agent today!

Ultra-Life Insurance is necessary.

Gelopolis Minor

Gelopolis Aquatis

Gelopolis Major

This is the exotic Gelopolis System. Once a forbidden region of extreme peril, it is now an ideal holiday destination. Since the Intergalactic Council certified the Gelopolis planets free from intelligent life, they are now yours to explore with only a minor risk to life and limb.

The Council welcomes both holiday makers and brave people (ideally those with scientific training) who are willing to settle on a far-off alien world.

INTERGALACTIC
COUNCIL

Gelopolis Minor

Gelopolis Minor is actively volcanic, with guaranteed eruptions every twenty minutes. The local wildlife is, of course, fireproof, and we recommend not spending more than half a day on the planet as the acidic air will slowly scorch your lungs away.

Think of the fun you can have with lava rapids, erupting volcanoes and a toxic landscape that will literally take your breath away!

ANIMAL FACT FILE

Often found lurking in shallow lava pools, the inferno frog is one of the more curious – and lethal – predators found on Gelopolis Minor. These critters are the size of a horse and belch boiling spittle to melt their prey into a sticky mess.

TOUR HIGHLIGHTS

Visit the magnificent Magma Falls, a cascading column of superheated rock that falls over 80 metres into a fiery pit. After a packed lunch and a chance to spot inferno frogs, the tour ends in the Flaming Jungles where brave guests can walk through the fire-resistant trees as the landscape spontaneously combusts around them.

Gelopolis Aquatis

Gelopolis Aquatis consists entirely of sea. With amazing marine life all around you, scuba-diving is a must. For sport fishing, why not try to catch the oblongo saw fish … before it catches you? Fun for all the family!

ANIMAL FACT FILE

The fifty-metre-long oblongo saw fish swim at incredible speed and use the rotating teeth along their noses to saw through anything – or anybody – in their way!

TOUR HIGHLIGHTS

Spend a day snorkelling in the tropical waters of this sun-kissed planet, exploring the massive coral reefs. You might even spot a pod of Gelopian ultra-whales, with their two tails and ability to speak up to three languages.

Enjoy an evening on a luxury floating beach, watching the sun sink across paradise, or snorkelling in the glowing kelp fields which come alive as darkness descends.

WHAT OUR GUESTS SAY ...

It was brilliant! The swimming was the best in the universe and my mum was terrified when an oblongo leapt out of the water and chopped our boat in half! We'll definitely come again!

Angus Warbler
(aged 12)

Gelopolis Major

Gelopolis Major is the largest planet in the system. Most of the landscape is a mix of desert scrubland and the famous Screaming Forests. Don't stray into the forests, as some plants there are smarter than you, and most can consume a person in one bite.

The abundance of life on this planet is fascinating, but most has yet to be properly studied. Gelopolis Major is therefore ideal for scientific pioneers.

ANIMAL FACT FILE

The slothlorax is the iconic species of Gelopolis Major, made famous in the Fable of the Screaming Forest. It should be avoided at all costs due to its ferocious nature. Beyond the fable and a few survival books, little is known about the slothlorax, except that it has poor eyesight and no sense of smell, so it relies on vibrations to hunt for its meals.

WHAT OUR SCIENTISTS SAY ...

This is such a wild planet that you need great survival skills. Make a fire both day and night – this will keep away all but the hungriest slothlorax. The branches of the Screaming Forest's quiver trees tend to shriek when burned, so bring your own firewood if you don't want to attract unwelcome attention.

Travel Information

Weather throughout the Gelopolis System is hot, but bearable. Factor 100+ sun-cream is recommended. Consult weather reports before travelling on Gelopolis Minor due to frequent flame tornados and scorching hurricanes, which are more common in the winter months.

Nobody is allowed on Gelopolis Aquatis if they can't swim or – due to unusual water chemistry – if they have a peanut allergy.

Luxury guided tours can be booked through Arm 'n' Leg Travel, while travellers on a tighter budget can get a great deal with Skint Exploration.

2132

Skint Exploration

SUMMER 2132

Arm 'n' Leg
T R A V E L

CRASH LANDING
Chapter 2

Chapter 2

Amber woke with a start and found that Baxter
had put his hand over her mouth to stop her
from screaming.

"It's a slothlorax," Baxter hissed.

The creature was huge, about the size of a
bull, but with a hammer-shaped head and a
fiercely fanged mouth big enough to consume
them in a single bite.

"Don't move," Baxter whispered. "They're almost blind but can detect vibrations." He was glad he remembered the key survival tips from his books, not to mention the old fable their mother had told them.

The beast paused, distracted by the dying pops and crackles of the burning branches. Within moments, the flames would fizzle out and Amber and Baxter would be on the menu. They had to do something.

Moving slowly, fearful of attracting the slothlorax's attention, Baxter picked up the fragment of metal he'd taken from the wreckage. It had looked fearsome when he chose it, but now he could see it wouldn't do anything more than annoy the creature.

With all his might, Baxter hurled the metal as far as he could over the creature's head. As it clattered against a tree, the slothlorax spun around with a mighty bellow and charged towards the noise.

With not a second to spare, Baxter yanked Amber to her feet and shoved her in the opposite direction.

"Run!"

He glanced behind in time to see the slothlorax's head cleave through a tree with such force the trunk snapped in half, and with it came a mighty scream from the plant that sent the surrounding branches violently quivering. The sudden movement from the trees all around them confused the beast, giving the children enough time to escape.

When they finally stopped to catch their breath, the slothlorax was far behind, as was the screaming forest.

"The trees," Baxter said as he caught his breath. "They scream, just like in the fable!"

Amber nodded. "Yep. I suggest we don't stop
and smell the flowers!"

Her expression sent Baxter into a fit of
giggles. When he finally calmed down he told
her about his dream. He saw her eyes widening
as her memories came back.

"D ... do you think Mum and Dad survived?"
Amber could barely get the words out.

"Absolutely. And I reckon they're not far
away."

Amber scanned the moonlit landscape.
"They could be anywhere!" It seemed like an
impossible task – to search an entire world to
find two people.

"Hang on – *now* I remember – Dad gave me a tracking token," said Amber. She reached into her pocket for the plain blue token and tossed it into the air. The gizmo glowed as it slowly floated across the savannah at walking pace. The children cautiously followed, aware that another slothlorax might be lurking in the darkness.

The token occasionally zigzagged to avoid perilous terrain, and the children knew that with every step they were drawing nearer to their parents.

Baxter wondered in what condition they'd find them. Injured? Or worse? The asteroid impact had been sudden and brutal. The fact that he and his sister had crash-landed in one piece was a miracle. Was it too much to hope their parents might have survived too?

Several times they heard movement in the darkness and braced themselves in case it was another slothlorax. But nothing attacked them, so they continued to follow the glowing token.

Dawn erupted over the horizon in a fierce fanfare of light from the dual suns, and with it the children could see a column of thick black smoke ahead, like an ink stain on the blue sky.

Drawing closer, they made out a shape near the source of the smoke. Another escape shuttle! This one had made a better landing than their own and didn't look damaged. The smoke came from a large bonfire to the side. Even at this distance they could see their parents throwing whatever they could remove from the shuttle to burn, sending up a signal to attract their children.

As Amber and Baxter sprinted towards their parents they could see that their father was on crutches, which meant he had been unable to venture into the wilderness to find them. Their mother rushed to hug them both, sobbing with relief.

Baxter was relieved too. He had no doubt that now they were back together, they would soon be able to leave this terrifying alien planet and head for safer worlds ...

Amazing Achievements

BY JOANNA NADIN

Setting the scene

In this text you will read a series of short biographies of different people. Some are from history and some are still alive today, but the one thing they all have in common is that they overcame obstacles and achieved incredible things. Each one has had an impact on the world and inspired other people.

Amazing Achievements

Some people are so determined and inspired that they have accomplished amazing things in spite of significant obstacles. These obstacles include medical conditions and attitudes to their race or gender. These people are truly remarkable and their achievements are heroic, because they have refused to let anything stop them in their determination to succeed.

Marie Curie

Marie Curie was born in Poland in 1867, the youngest of five children of impoverished school-teacher parents. After her mother died, Marie became a governess to earn money, but she read constantly in her spare time. She eventually moved to Paris where she studied physics and maths, and married scientist Pierre Curie. Together they conducted ground-breaking research into radioactivity; research that now helps us beat cancer.

Marie and Pierre Curie

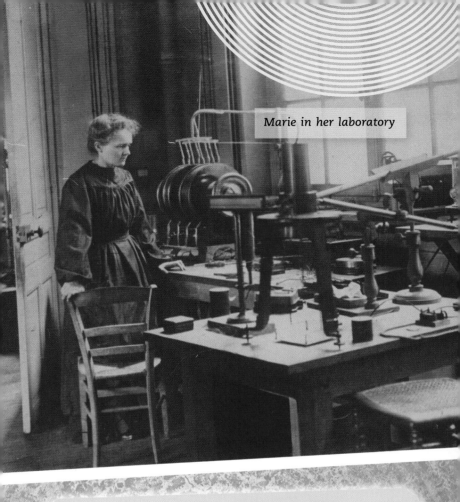
Marie in her laboratory

This work made Marie the first woman to win the **Nobel Prize**. After Pierre died, Marie became the first person ever to win the prize twice, after discovering ways to measure radioactivity. This is an astonishing achievement in a world and profession dominated by men.

Thomas Edison

Born in 1847, Thomas Edison was an American scientist and inventor whose work on inventions, such as the electric light bulb and the film camera, changed the world. As a child, he suffered from scarlet fever and ear infections which left him with severe hearing difficulties. This made it hard for him to learn at school, but his teachers simply thought he was being difficult.

Thomas Edison celebrating the lightbulb's 50th anniversary in 1929.

His mother took him out of school and taught him at home instead. This was the making of him. By the age of twelve, Thomas had set up a business printing and selling newspapers on the railways, and he also began conducting experiments. The rest, as they say, is history.

DID YOU KNOW?

Stephen Hawking is a British physicist and mathematician who suffers from motor neurone disease, a condition which causes muscle paralysis. Despite this, he continues to make many important discoveries about the laws which govern the universe. He is probably the most famous scientist of our era.

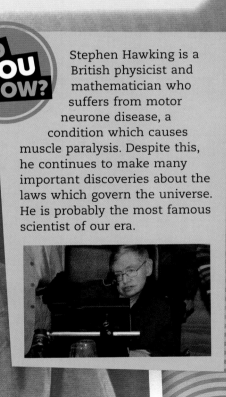

Helen Keller

Born in 1880, Helen Keller reportedly started speaking at just six months old. However, a year later, she caught what was then called a 'brain fever' – possibly scarlet fever or meningitis – which left her deaf and blind. This didn't stop Helen trying to communicate, but her attempts were limited, and her behaviour became bad, possibly through frustration.

Helen Keller with her teacher Anne Sullivan

Helen Keller in later life

Helen's mother didn't give up hope, and hired a teacher called Anne Sullivan. Anne taught Helen to communicate using sign language, and Helen eventually learned to use **Braille** too. Thanks to her own determination, and Anne's, Helen went on to become an author, political activist and lecturer.

Barack Obama

Barack Obama was born in Hawaii in 1961 to a black father and white mother, at a time when race relations in America were strained. After his parents divorced, 'Barry', as he was then known, was brought up partly by his mother, and partly by his grandparents in Hawaii.

Barack Obama speaking in North Carolina, July 2016

The easy-going, **multicultural** life in Hawaii gave Barack his values and vision of a world in which people respect each other. At college, he began campaigning to improve people's lives. In 2008, he made history when he became America's first black president.

DID YOU KNOW?

The first African American to serve in the US government was Hiram Rhodes Revels, who became senator for Mississippi in 1870. This is a remarkable achievement, as many black people were slaves when he was born, and slavery wasn't abolished in America until 1865.

Malala Yousafzai

Born in Pakistan in 1997, Malala Yousafzai began blogging about her life when she was eleven, raising issues like girls' right to an education. In 2011, when she was fourteen years old, Malala was awarded Pakistan's first National Youth Peace Prize. The Taliban, a group of violent extremists who saw women and girls as second-class citizens, reacted furiously to her promotion of girls' rights to education.

In response to her rising fame, they decided to kill her and, in October 2012, a masked gunman climbed on to her schoolbus and shot her in the head.

Malala Yousafzai receiving the Nobel Prize for Peace

Incredibly, Malala survived and was brought to England to recover. Instead of being silenced, she condemned her attackers and campaigned even more widely for women's and girls' rights. In 2014, she became the youngest person ever to receive the Nobel Prize for Peace, donating the prize money to build a school for girls in Pakistan.

Glossary

Braille a way of writing using raised dots, which blind people can read by feeling with their fingertips

multicultural containing several ethnic groups

Nobel Prize a famous prize given to people who have achieved something outstanding

DARE TO BE DIFFERENT

BY JOANNA NADIN

ILLUSTRATED BY ALEX PATERSON

Setting the scene

Do you enjoy dancing? Have you ever had any dancing lessons? Ballet is a type of dancing which involves learning how to jump, turn and hold different positions. All the dance moves have French names such as *jeté* (a jump), *pirouette* (a spin on one foot), *plié* (a bend from the knees) and *arabesque* (standing on one leg with the other leg behind you, arms stretched out). Ballet dancers need to be very fit and strong.

Chapter 1

Manjit Jones was good at a lot of things. He could skateboard nearly as well as the Norton twins, who were famous round town for their kickflips and ollies, and he could run nearly as fast as Pete Prendergast, who had once won the all-county under-elevens sprint. Best of all, he could keep his football in the air nearly as long as his best mates Marv and Sanjay, who had been the stars of the school playground for three weeks running.

Yes, Manjit Jones was good at a lot of things. But he was only excellent at one thing.

This thing was a secret. A secret so big that it would skid the Norton twins off their skateboards. A secret so enormous it would trip Pete Prendergast up in his tracks. A secret so surprising it would flip Marv's and Sanjay's footballs sideways.

The secret was ballet.

It had started when Manjit was made to go with his dad to watch his big sister Saffron in her ballet school's Dance Extravaganza.

"Do I have to?" he'd moaned. "None of my friends are going, and besides, ballet's *boring*."

Dad had been livid. "Boring?" he demanded. "Bet you can't do the splits or stand on your toes for hours on end. Ballet dancers are some of the fittest athletes about. Way fitter than footballers, I'll warrant."

Manjit wasn't convinced, but he'd known better than to argue with his dad, so he'd sighed a secret sigh and gone along to Miss Blister's Ballet Academy with a comic under his coat to while away the time.

However, a funny thing had happened as soon as the lights went down. Instead of reaching for his pocket torch and copy of *Captain Invincible*, Manjit found himself mesmerized by what was happening on stage. As the girls danced, he noticed that his feet were twitching and his legs itching to follow each step.

"Did you enjoy that, then?" his dad had asked afterwards.

"I suppose," said Manjit.

"You could always have a go yourself," suggested his dad. "Only if you wanted."

"Maybe," said Manjit.

Manjit decided he would have a go. From that day onwards, he'd been tagging along with his sister twice a week and was the rising star of Miss Blister's. He'd sworn Saffron and her friends to secrecy though, and his dad too. There was no way he wanted Marv and Sanjay or anyone else to know what he was doing.

Not ever.

Or so he told himself. Until one day in June when Manjit and his mates saw a poster that had been pinned up on the school notice board.

'Dare to be Different Talent Show' it read.
'Show the whole school your secret skill and
win a VIP trip for six to Superior Minds Science
Park. Friday at 3pm in the hall.'

"I'm going to do keepy-uppy with my football,"
said Marv. "I'll do a hundred in a row!"

"Me too," said Sanjay. "Only I'll do two
hundred!"

"What about you, Manjit?" asked Marv.

"Yeah," said Sanjay. "What're you going to do?"

Manjit felt his face redden at the thought of
his secret skill. "Keepy-uppy, I suppose," he said,
"but I don't reckon I'll beat either of you two."

Marv and Sanjay shrugged. They knew it was
true, but didn't want to say it.

"Hopefully one of us will win anyway," said Sanjay.

"Yeah, one of us," said Marv. "Then we'll all go on the prize trip together, hey?"

"Definitely," said Manjit. "Good plan."

It was a good plan, but Manjit knew there was definitely no way it would be him who won for the boys. Not unless ...

*

"You've got to do it," said Dad.

Saffron nodded. "It's time to show them who you really are," she said.

"But I'm really Manjit," said Manjit, "who skates and runs and plays football with his mates."

Dad smiled. "But there's another Manjit too, isn't there?"

Manjit nodded.

There was. There was the
Manjit who could *jeté* higher
than Julie Cooper. The Manjit who
could *pirouette* and *plié* more precisely than Priya
Patel. The Manjit whose splits were more splendid
than his own sister's, and she didn't even mind
because she was so proud.

Manjit knew his dad and Saffron were right.

He had to be brave.

He had to be the Other Manjit.

In short, he had to dare to be different.

DARE TO BE DIFFERENT
Chapter 2

Chapter 2

Manjit peeked from behind the curtain. The school hall was teeming with pupils, parents and teachers too. He felt his knees tremble and his stomach lurch and slide. He must be mad to even consider doing this!

Just then he felt a friendly slap on his back. He turned to see his mates Marv and Sanjay poised and ready in their kit, footballs in their hands.

The pair looked at Manjit.

"Where's your football shirt?" asked Sanjay.

"And your ball?" demanded Marv. "You'll need a ball."

"I ..." began Manjit. "I left them at home."

"No worries," said Sanjay. "You can borrow mine. I'll bring them to you when I'm done."

"Thanks," said Manjit. "But I'll be okay. I've ... got something else planned."

Sanjay and Marv frowned.

"What do you mean?" asked Marv.

"What else?" asked Sanjay.

Manjit took a deep breath. "You'll see," he said.

The other boys looked at each other, perplexed, but there was no time for more questions: the lights had dimmed and the curtain was about to go up.

First to perform was Marv, who managed ninety-two keepy-uppies. Up next was Sanjay who didn't drop his ball until he'd got to a hundred and thirteen. After Sanjay came Lucy Pooter who played the violin and only got two notes wrong; after Lucy came Hari Woo who did three backflips and a one-handed cartwheel; after Hari came Juno Bruce who recited all her times tables right up to thirteen; and after Juno came ...

"Manjit Jones." The head teacher, Mr Bonnett, called him on to the stage.

Manjit's legs were wobbling, but he steadied them with a stretch. "I can do this," he told himself.

Mr Bonnett called Manjit's name again, and pressed the button to start the music.

"What're you up to?" hissed Sanjay.

"Are you all right?" asked Marv.

Manjit nodded. "I hope so," he said. "I really hope so." This was it. There was no going back now. He had to be brave. He had to dare to be different ...

... and he did!

As the music from *Swan Lake* filled the hall, Manjit leapt out to centre stage before spinning to a standstill. Then he raised his arms in perfect fifth position and began his dance.

That afternoon, Manjit danced as he'd never danced before. His turns were tighter, his leaps were longer, and his *arabesque* was straighter and steadier than it had ever been. He could feel it too, so that by the time he got to his final *pirouette* he wasn't just performing, he was enjoying himself.

The audience was enjoying it as well. Manjit could see Dad and Saffron smiling in the second row, and behind them the Norton twins nodding their heads in appreciation. Best of all, when he glanced into the wings, Marv and Sanjay were both grinning broadly.

Then, as the music stopped, and Manjit came forward to take a bow, the crowd went wild. Everyone stood up and began cheering and clapping and shouting his name, "Manjit! Manjit! Manjit!"

Manjit bowed again. He could hardly believe it. Even Luke Rigby, who was second toughest in their year, was grinning and whistling and calling for more.

In the end Manjit managed two more *pirouettes* before Mr Bonnett had to ask him to leave the stage because Olivia Hooper wanted to play her ukulele. He didn't stop glowing with pride all afternoon and evening ...

... and all the next day, when he took Sanjay and Marv, and Dad and Saffron, and Saffron's friend Suki to Superior Minds Science Park.

"I can't believe you won," said Sanjay as they watched Professor Potts explode sodium in a special private show.

"I can," said Marv, "but I can't believe you kept it a secret for so long. Why didn't you tell us?"

"I thought you'd laugh at me," admitted Manjit.

"No way," said Marv.

"Yeah, why would you think that?" asked Sanjay.

Manjit shrugged. "Just because it's ... different, I suppose."

"I suppose," said Sanjay.

"So, footy later?" asked Marv. "Or have you gone off that?"

"No," said Manjit. "I'll just send the Other Manjit round instead."

Sanjay and Marv looked at each other, then back at Manjit. "You okay?" they asked.

Manjit smiled and pointed his toes. "I am," he said. "I really am."